Julia's Model Series

:Lauren:
Sensuality of Form

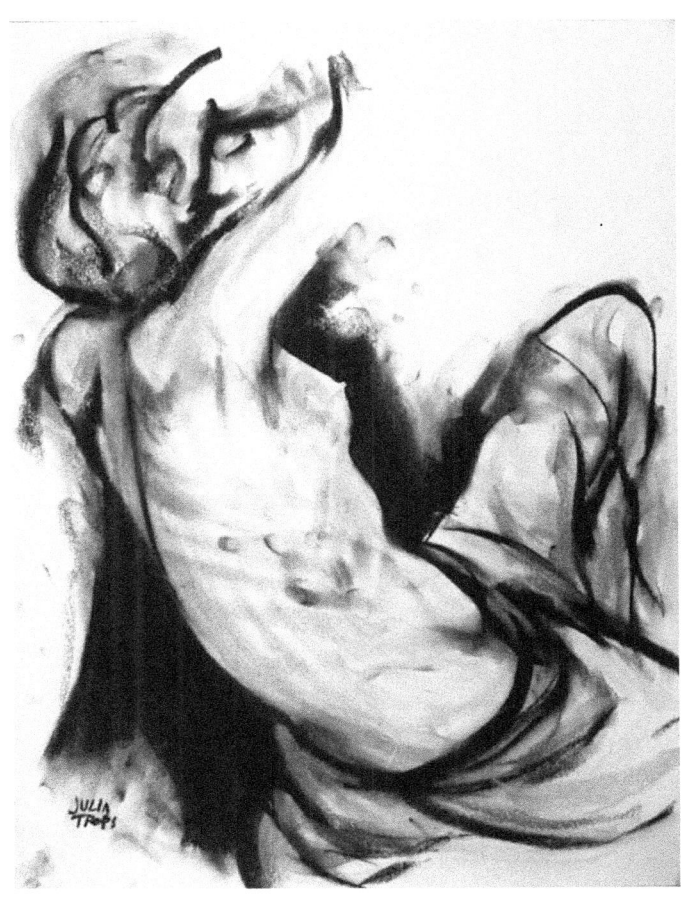

by Julia Trops

Published by Julia Trops ISBN 978-0-9813363-0-5

Designed and written by Julia Trops

Cover artwork Lauren by Julia Trops.

font: title page: Verdana
paragraphs and headings: Adobe Garamond

A heartfelt thank you....

to Lauren,

my model, but more importantly,
my loyal and very supportive friend.

and to Greg Riley - an amazing Chicago artist and friend, who
proofread and edited for me, and pointed out how much I love
quotes and dashes and paranthesesestes. It was - fun!!
(Seriously, it was.)

Introduction

I am most completely enraptured with the essence of the female symbol as described through comparative mythology. Each culture of the world integrates the female symbol in many similar ways. Ultimately, the female is the symbol of creative spirit in all her forms - both creative and destructive, erotic and matronly, (and who says these are not interchangeable?)

While each of my models have within a summary of all of these types, each model has one quality that seems to stand higher than all the rest. Each book in this series will focus on a specific quality seen in each model: for Lauren, this quality is sensuality.

Contents

Background

Just like any other artist, I've always drawn - I can't remember a day when I haven't. Music and song have been my escape, and dance has been a passion even though I sound like a crow and am completely uncoordinated. In my mind, I sing and dance perfectly!

I was encouraged from a very young age to see and be aware in more ways than the visual. Immediately after high school I took courses in the University of Calgary Fine Arts program. I continued studies at a post secondary level throughout my 12 year career in the Canadian Air Force, in both correspondence and night school. One of my ultimate goals was finally reached when I attended a full time degree program at University of Lethbridge, receiving a Bachelor of Fine Arts with Great Distinction in 2001.

In 2002, we moved to Kelowna, and in competition with 78 other candidates, I was chosen to be one of 6 resident artists in the new Rotary Centre for the Arts. I am still there today.

Among the historical art influences on my work are the artists of the Greek classical, da Vinci, Rembrandt, Ingres, Delacroix, Manet, Van Gogh, Cezanne, Matisse, Picasso, Tapies, and most recently, Klee and Kandinsky.

Influences from art theory include John Berger, Josef Albers, from theosophy include Leadbetter and Blavatsky, Fritjof Capra and currently Joseph Campbell.

I never really know what to expect when I walk in to a drawing class - I only know who the model is, and depending on the vibes of that day, I will choose my tools.

Usually, I will bring an assortment of mediums, from charcoal and graphite, to ink, and the paper is fairly reliable being the kraft paper, and cartridge, with I fell in love with in 2006. When a really special pose presents itself, and all the magic is there, I will use the special Somerset Velvet paper, or the watercolour paper, or the mango leaf paper. But the vibes have to be right and in sync.

I am very organized, and focused when I create work. I think this is a very valuable set of skills developed while I was working in the Canadian Air Force. The goal was clear, the tools were present, and so was I. It has always seemed fairly effortless.

I am a big reader, self-study is my way of life. I am brought to mind the anonymous quote "Give a man a fish; you have fed him for today. Teach a man to fish; and you have fed him for a lifetime". I am a fisherman.

I realized in 2006 that I was a minimalist - an artist who was looking for the most simple, direct expression possible without any tanglements of ego or self, but with the echoes of continued vibrational energies afterwards. I know I could never remove self completely, but from about that time, I was looking for artwork that would stand by itself, and be independent of the artist.

2007

In 2007, I did maybe about 1000 to 1100 works. About 100 of those were oil and acrylic paintings, nine were bronze medallions, and the rest were charcoal and ink works. The focus was on the balance of light and dark and the philosophical meaning of the pushing of the light and dark against each other. Was there a battle going on within? I am not sure, I just knew that there was no reason to be afraid of the dark, and I pushed the boundaries of the creation of form, and the battle of good and evil, as each edge touched and encroached upon the other.

Whether I was looking for the darkness within myself or the model, is up for debate, perhaps both, but I knew from my experience with depression that as much as I could feel pain, I could feel that much joy. There is a balance in all things and the pendulum swings one way and then the next.

According to our western mythologies, we live in a dualistic world, but by choice, we can be free of these restrictions. I think out of anything I studied in 2007, this realization, as written about by Joseph Campbell, had the most impact, and was the most influential on my work at that time.

In Campbell's book, Power of Myth, on page 66, he states: "One of the problems of life is to live with the realization of both terms, to say "I know the centre, and I know that good and evil are simply temporal abberations that , in God's view, there is no difference".

There does exist somewhere a perfect balance, a stillness, a stop where all things are equal, where all exists and nothing exists. This is where I try to go and to express in my work, and I know which works are a result of this place, the "noble silence".

Probably the most influential text of 2005, was the Tao of Physics by Fritjof Capra. From page 180: "The Eastern mystics link the notions of both space and time to particular states of consciousness. Being able to go beyond the ordinary state through meditation, they have realized that the coventional notions are of space and time are not the ultimate truth. ... The discovery that all space and time measurements are relative."

There was a point where I tried to remove the element of time from my work. I was working on becoming efficient, removing the element of ego and conscious awareness (the watcher) from any markmaking I did. Some call this meditation, and indeed it was a form of trance that I could impose, sometimes at will. With practice, it certainly became easier.

There was a point, I think, in 2007, where I felt I had arrived at this form of meditation, and even moved beyond the element of being an artist. I had become a conductor of sorts, a conductor of medium, of shape and form. I was not present as I waved my charcoal baton and the drawing appeared, a valid expression of sight and sound.

About Lauren

by Lauren Wilson

How I started modelling was by chance. I was attending a Livessence drawing session and it just happened we were stuck without a model so I volunteered. Why I chose to continue modelling was much more deeply rooted.

Years ago in my fine arts studies at college, as a young terribly insecure 18 year old, I always wondered in the back of my mind if I could ever be so bold, so confident, so comfortable within myself to life model. I so enjoyed the process of drawing the figure from life and admired the models ability to provide the energy and the spark from which I could then connect with and build upon to create a dynamic drawing.

Another 18 years later, I finally had the chance to test that question of "Can I do that?". Modelling has brought me immense rewards in confidence, connection with artists, and another outlet to express myself creatively.

I take pride in being a life model, in being a part of a creative process, and of having the confidence and comfort within myself to do so.

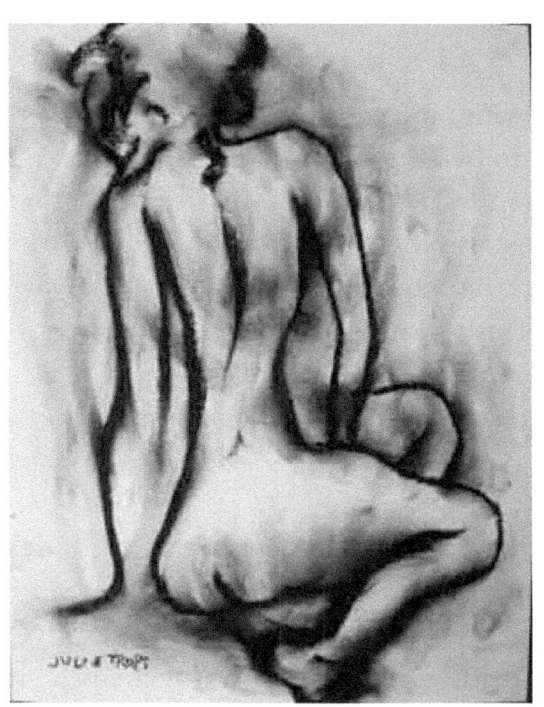

With Lauren....

With Lauren, I saw the struggle between light and dark, the struggle between feminity and the denial of the same. I saw a searching, a life on the journey to self-discovery. I saw myself in her mirror.

I saw a fluctuating, mesmerizing solid strength an instant later blurring to become delicate transparent skin. I felt she was a spirit manifest, but there was a struggle that went on within was completely captivating. Sensuality to me means with all the senses, and when I was drawing Lauren, I connected in this way.

I could see the creative potential and was anxious to bring it out.

When I first met Lauren, in 2004, we had no idea she would be modelling with me three years later. I am very glad she did. Knowing her for that length of time has given a depth to the artworks and a full realization of the potential of the sensual being she held within.

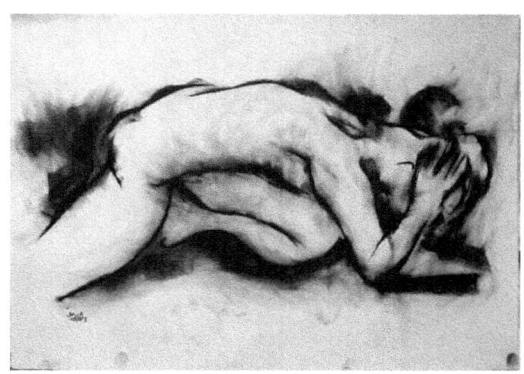

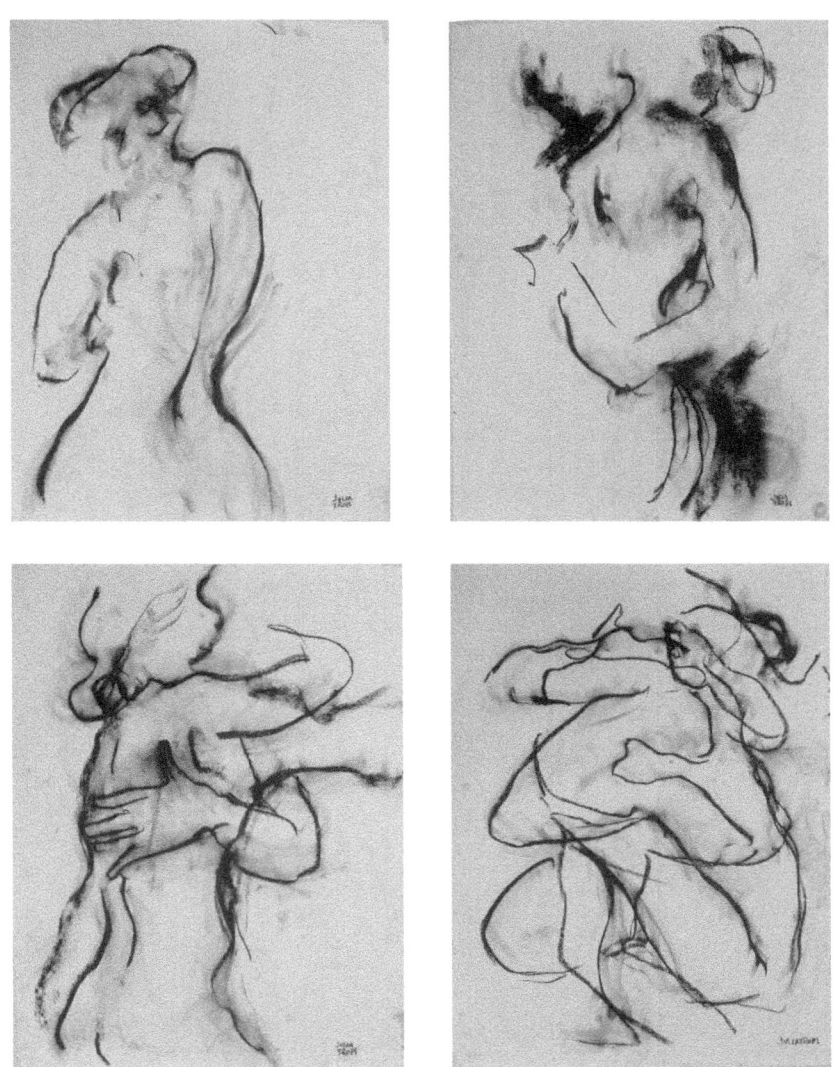

Gesture drawings, 5-20 seconds poses
Charcoal on cartridge or Canson paper

The Okanagan Erotic Art Show

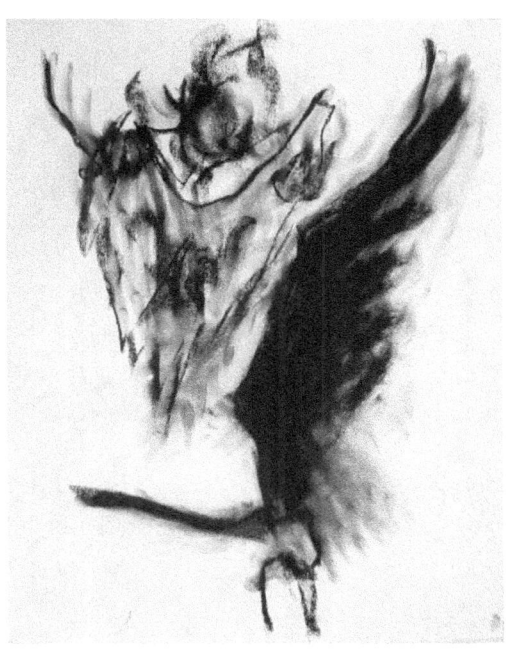

When I first came to Kelowna in 2002, and became an artist in the Rotary Centre, a few of my nudes on display were turned to the wall.

One evening during the Life and Arts Festival, my two friends, Angie and Lauren, and I were having a glass of wine while we were manning the Livessence booth.

"Wouldn't it be fun if..."

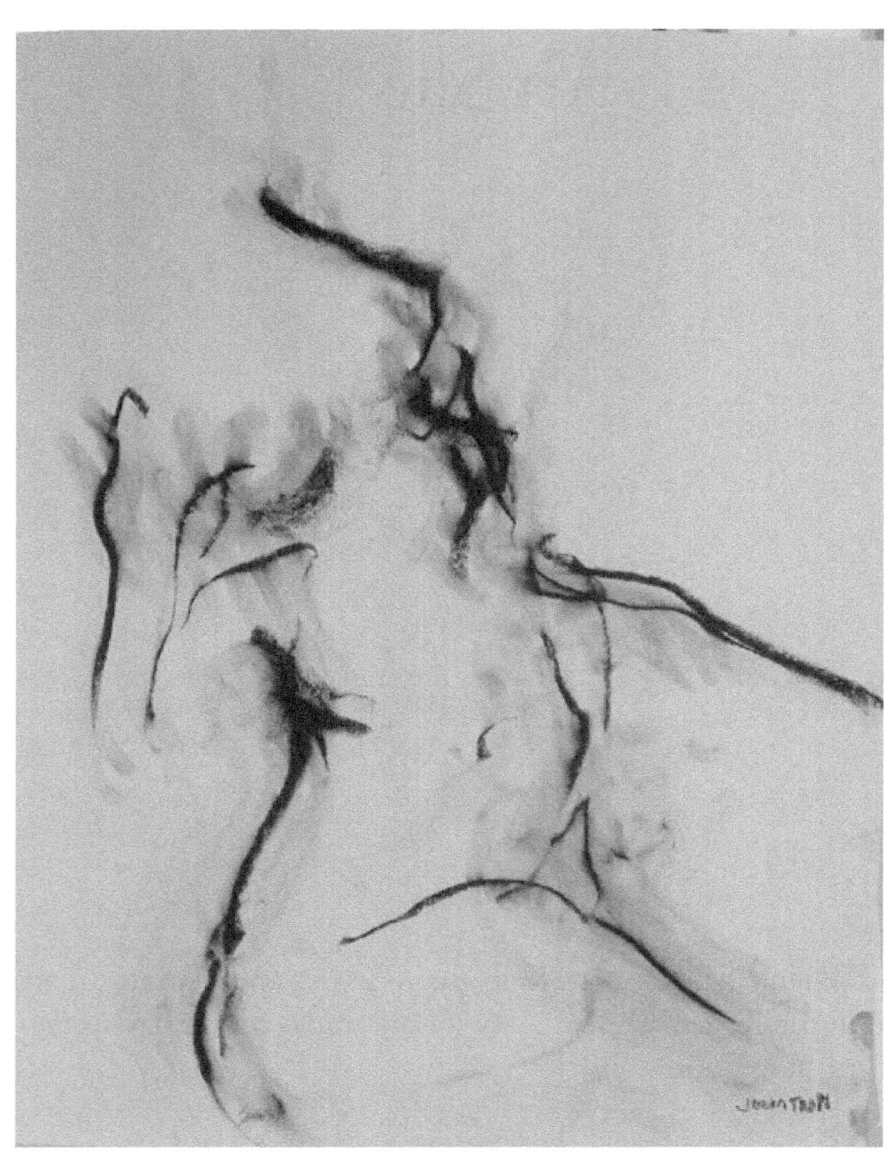

Charcoal on paper, 24x18

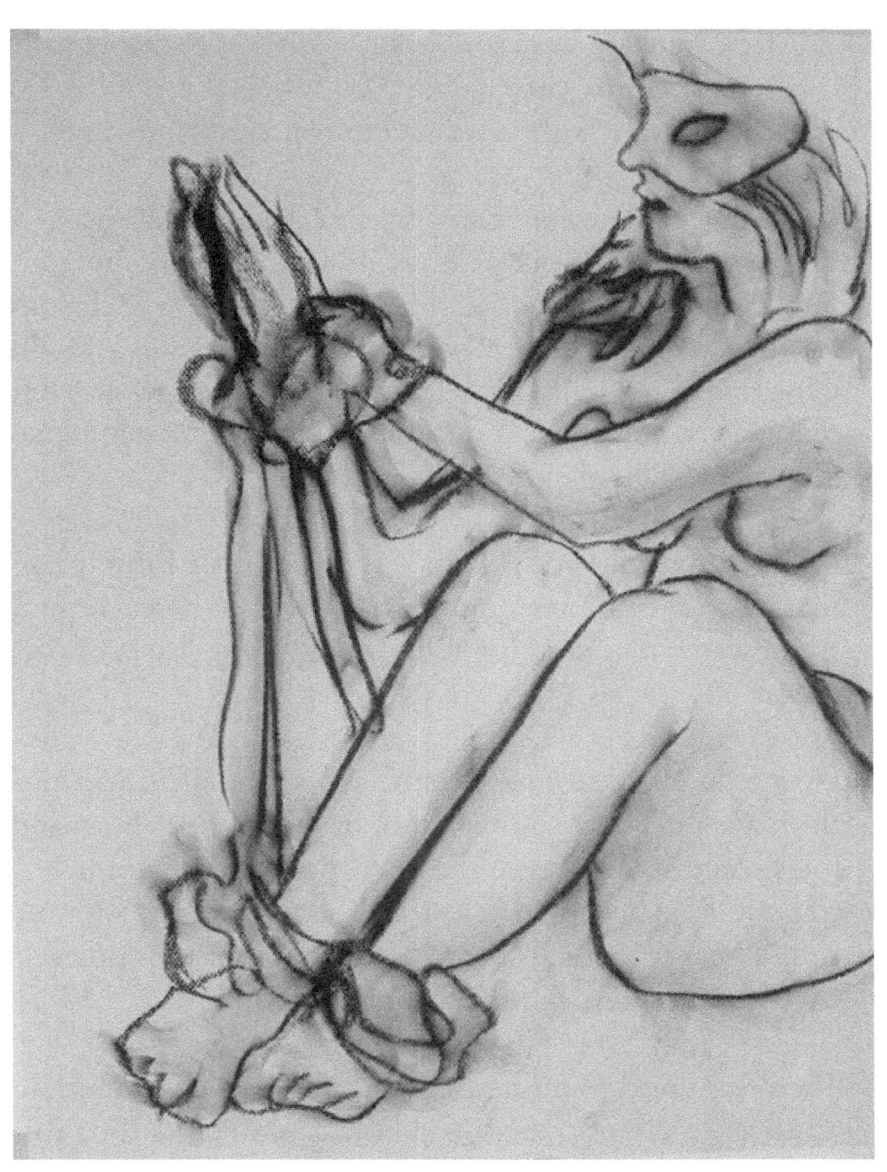

Charcoal on paper, 24x18

Truth be told, we were somewhat (okay, more than a little) frustrated that the current accepted forms of art in this small town were fairly restricted to fruit and landscapes.

Very few people would come by and even look at the figurative art on display. We would watch them point fingers at the work and talk in hushed voices. We felt sorry for these people who obviously had never been in an Italian Church or on a french beach. We had quite a few glasses of red wine by this time, and I don't remember how loud we got with our discussion!

We each agreed that the female form (or male form, for that matter) could be found in fruit, such as pears, or in a landscape of undulating hills or the rolling waves of the water.

How could we make people, the general public understand this? Well, hell, we said, why not have an erotic show, and folks could see how even the lowly pear or the knot in a tree could be perceived as erotic. The focus of the show of course, was to get across the idea that eroticism is on the part of the viewer, and their sole responsibility.

Then we agreed to meet after the Life and Arts exhibition was over to discuss details and how we could get the Erotic show on the road.

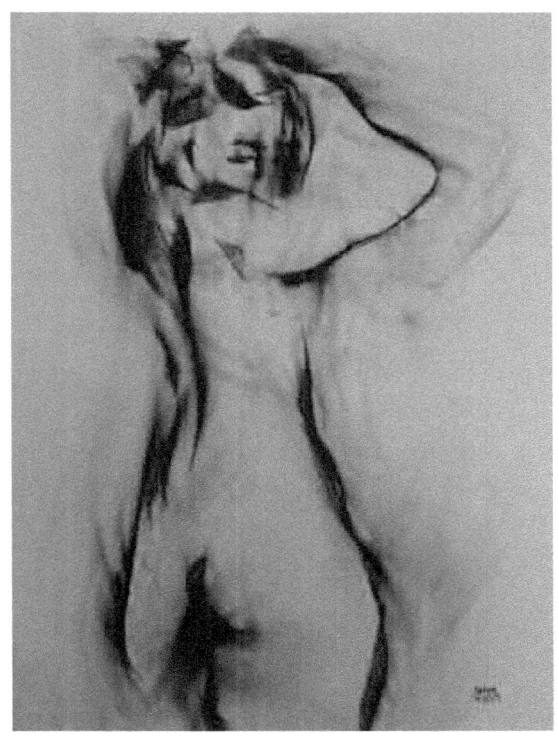

We met in August and September, had some brainstorming sessions of how we would approach this, how open the show would be, where and when it would be and the types of artists we could send to.

We also wanted this to be separate from the current Livessence drawing sessions to differentiate between the normal life drawing and eroticism. We made arrangements with models to add a bit of spice to some specially arranged drawing sessions, and Lauren was one of those models.

Accroutements such as shoes, masks, scarves, sheer fabric and beaded collars were added. These drawing sessions were open to all artists who wanted to attend.

The first Call to Artists went out in October 2007, and we received so many interesting submissions, some humourous such as Iris Morden's codpieces to the gorgeous pastels of Katherine Upton. The show became valley wide, and actually extended slightly beyond the valley in to Kamloops.

Our first Erotic show, held at the Rotary Centre for the Arts in March/April 2008, we felt was extremely successful. It received publicity from Sheryl McKay's CBC Radio's Vancouver broadcast North by Northwest, to write-ups in the newspaper, and Letters to the Editor protesting the display of artworks in the Rotary Centre for the Arts. We were pleased.

Since the Okanagan Erotic Art Show was on in the Rotary Centre for the Arts, no one's figurative art pieces have been turned to the wall. A few more local people have purchased figurative art and as of this writing, May 31 2009, the second Erotic Show is on it's way to becoming the talk of the town again this year.

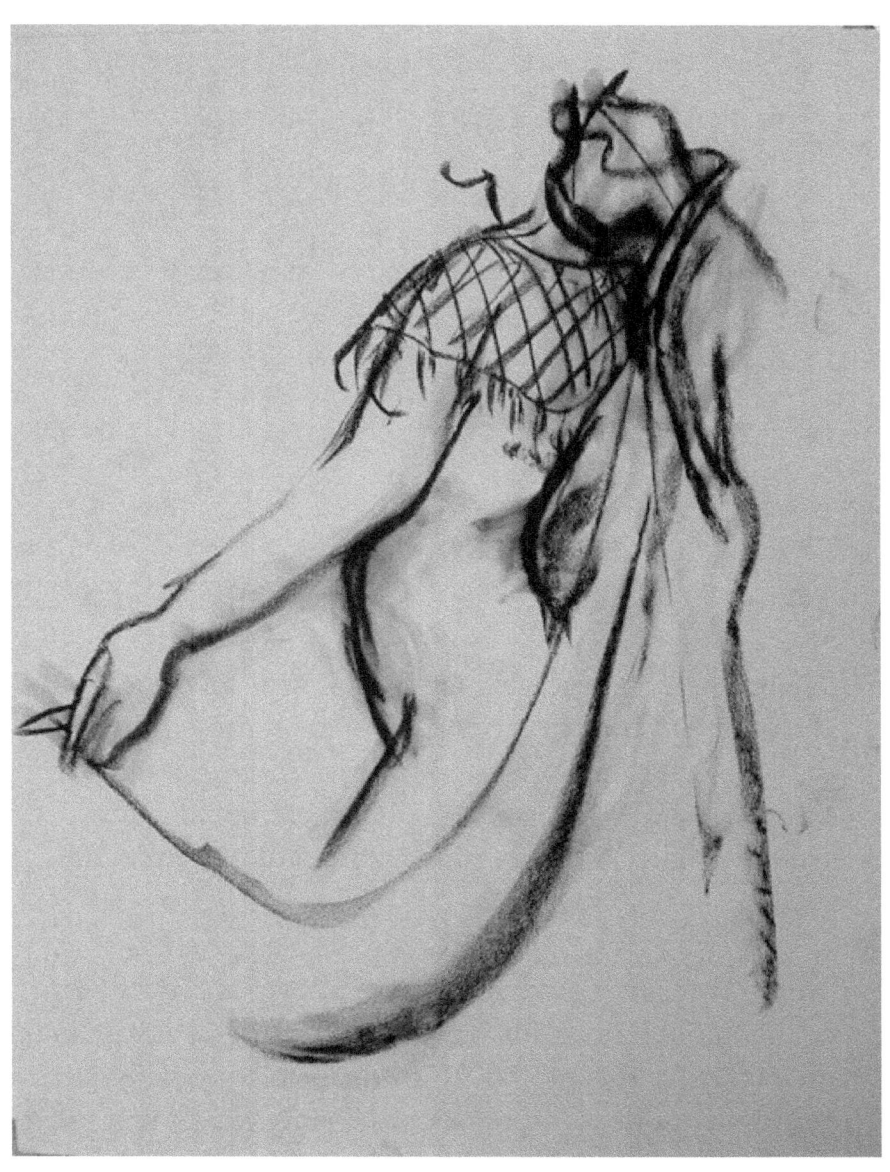

Gesture drawing
Charcoal on canson 26x20

2008

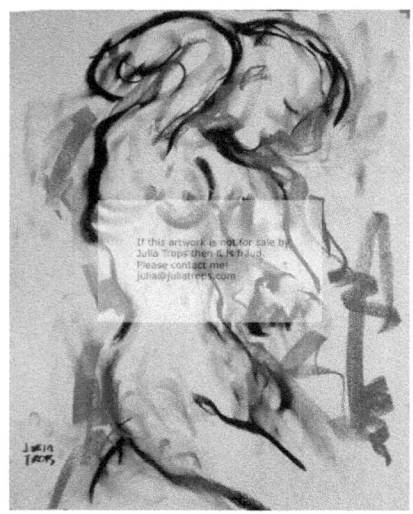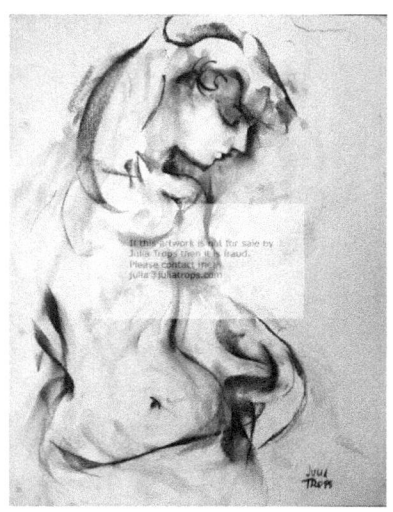

These works, on the next few pages, were all done from the same 2.5 hour session. All works on these pages are 24"x18" charcoal and the lovely responsive Schmincke pastels on cartridge paper, unless where noted. The palette is fairly limited to black, tan, pink, lavender and green.

You may see the same pose repeated over and over again as different elements of movement, energy and expression are tackled and explored. With the erotic show behind me, my confidence in my expression increased tenfold, and I am more fearless in my pursuit of sensual and sophisticated expression.

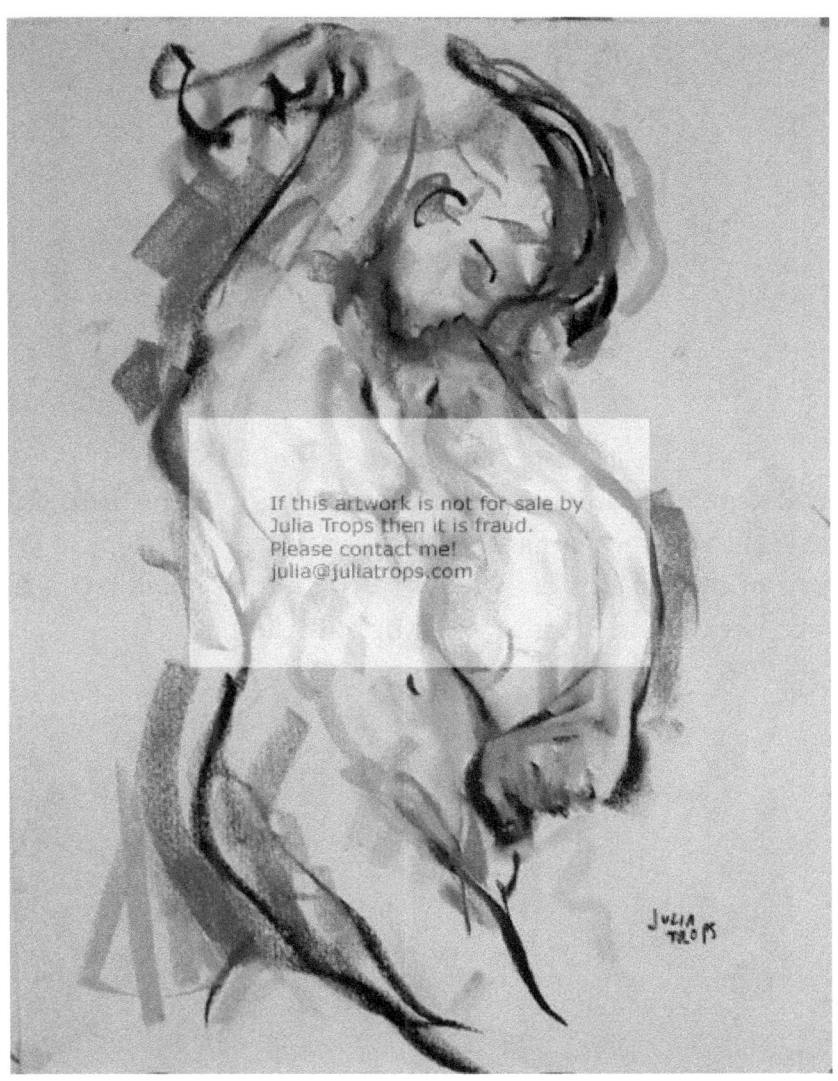

I will draw the same pose but arbitrarily move the arms and the legs to further enhance the expression. For this pose the focus of impact was on the left waist and the small triangle of space between the feet as they support the body.

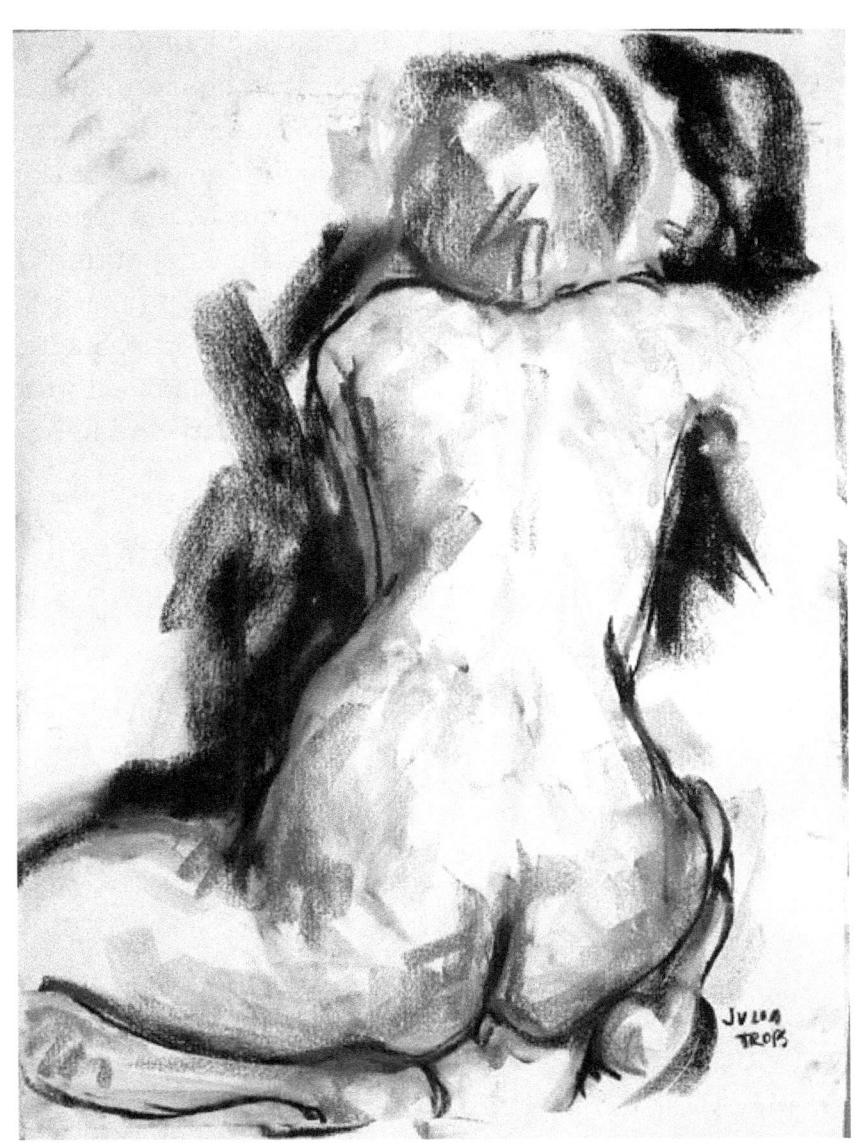

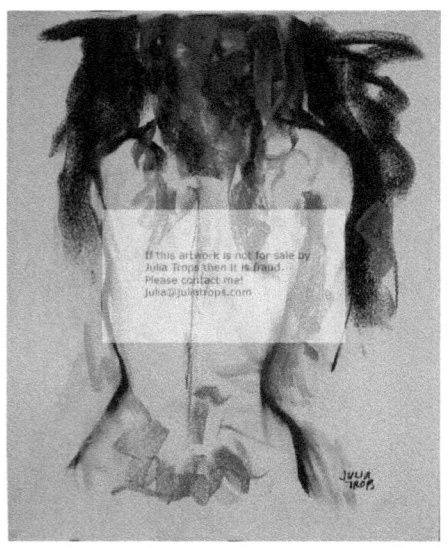

Sometimes the expression is completely on the balance of light and dark on the page. As the mark-making progresses, I am more aware of the action of the charcoal markings on the paper, and that becomes my focus. Such was the case here, with the balance of dark and light.

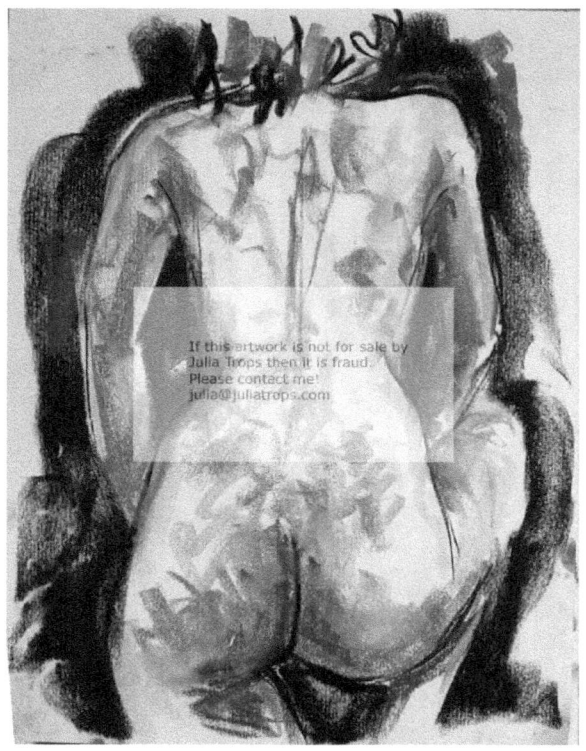

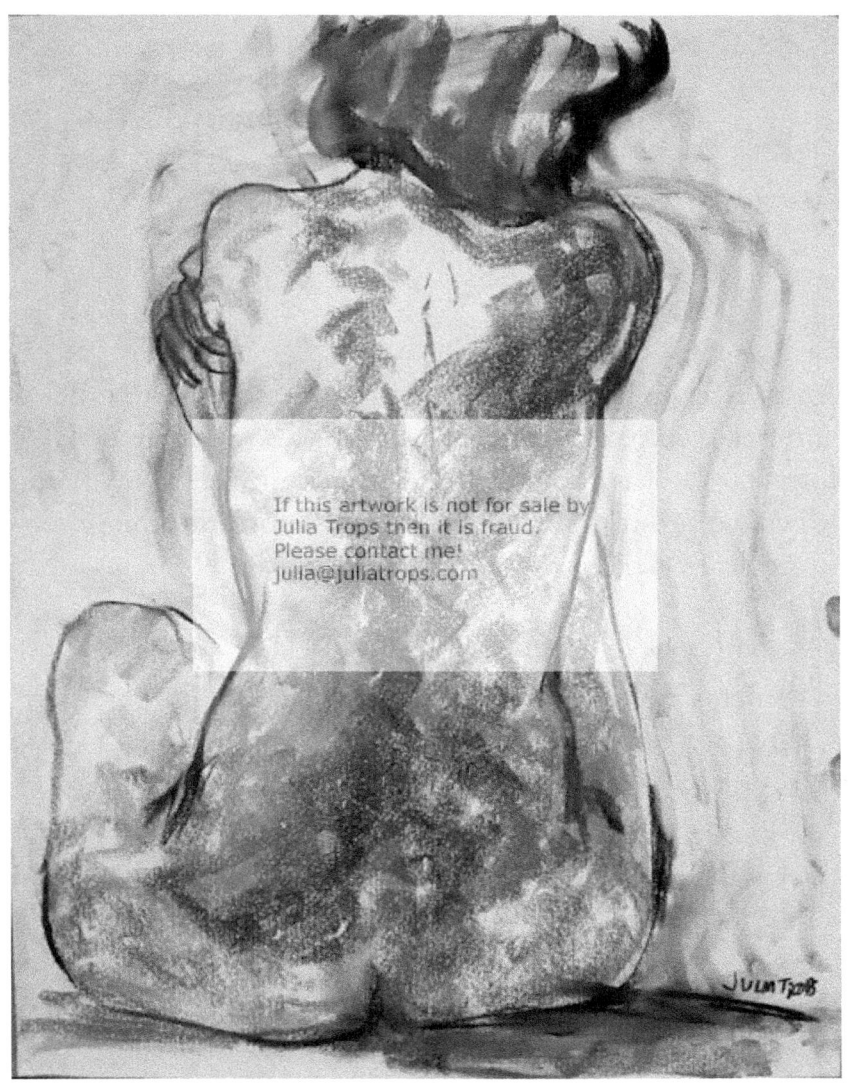

I was really enjoying the play of shadows across Lauren's form in this pose, and the undulations of the outside edges. Like water flowing, the charcoal moved and the pastel followed.

And there are times, when the pose is so classical and Greek and beautiful that I can not help but draw it. The time for this one was about ten minutes complete, as my hands moved without my conscious brain. I consider the process successful when I can reach that place.

This palette is very limited, with pale pink, pale green and lavender, with some reds, and browns on the kraft paper. Unabashed feminine beauty, a suggestion and hint of colour.

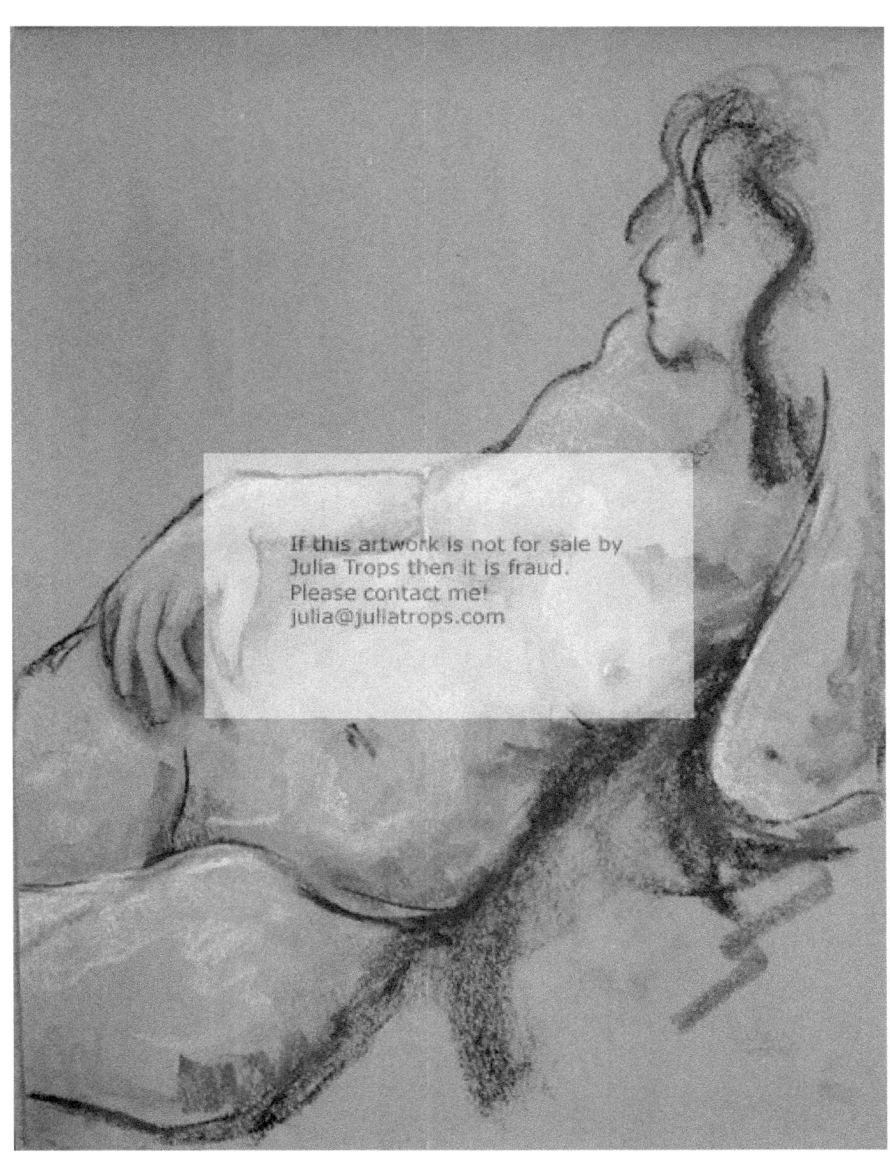

Charcoal and Schmincke pastel on 24"x18" kraft paper

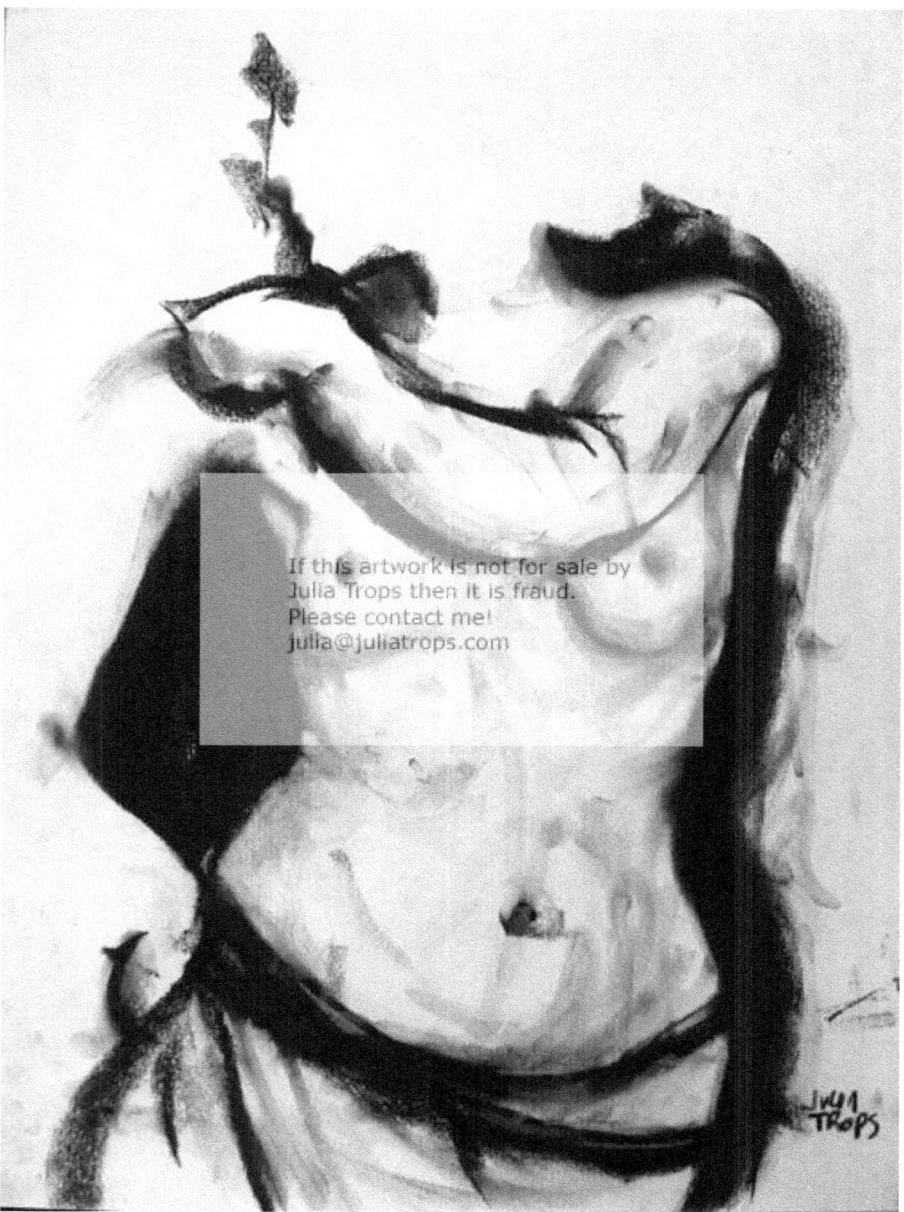

If this artwork is not for sale by
Julia Trops then it is fraud.
Please contact me!
julia@juliatrops.com

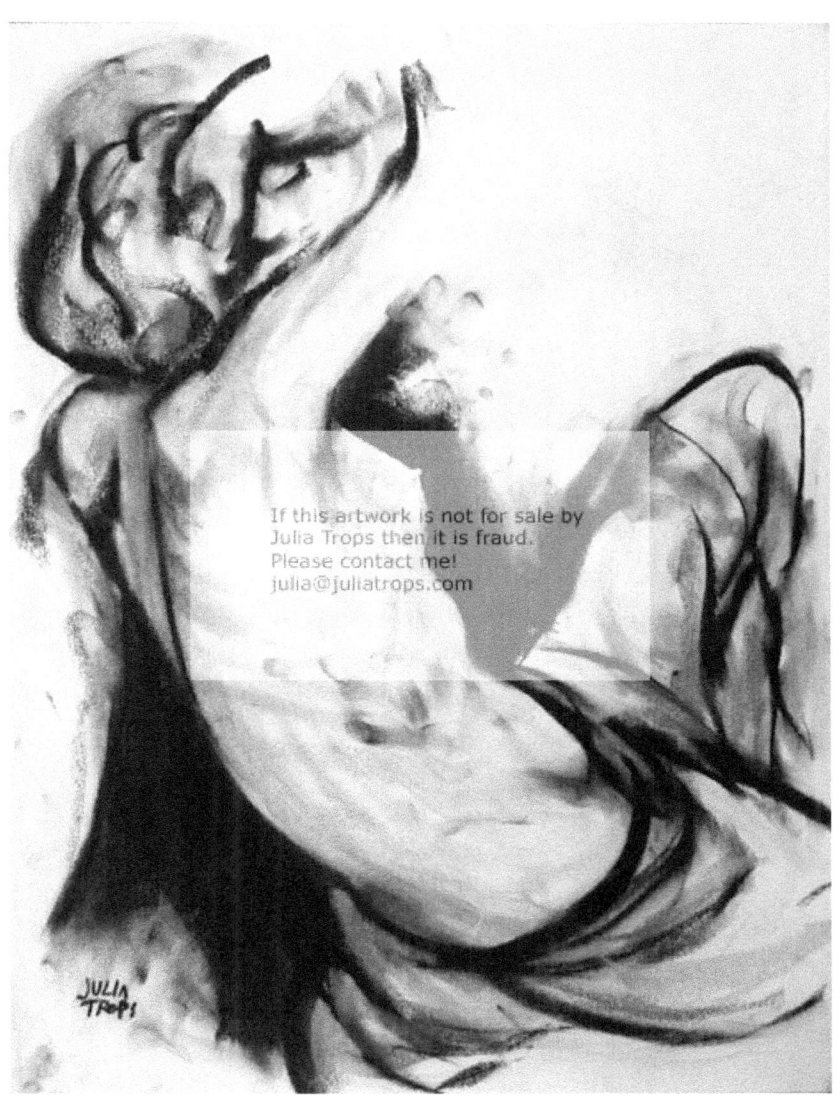

Lovely shadows and subtle textures with the limited palette. By now, the lavender and pink and green have become symbols of gentle grace when placed amongst the harsh reality of the charcoal.

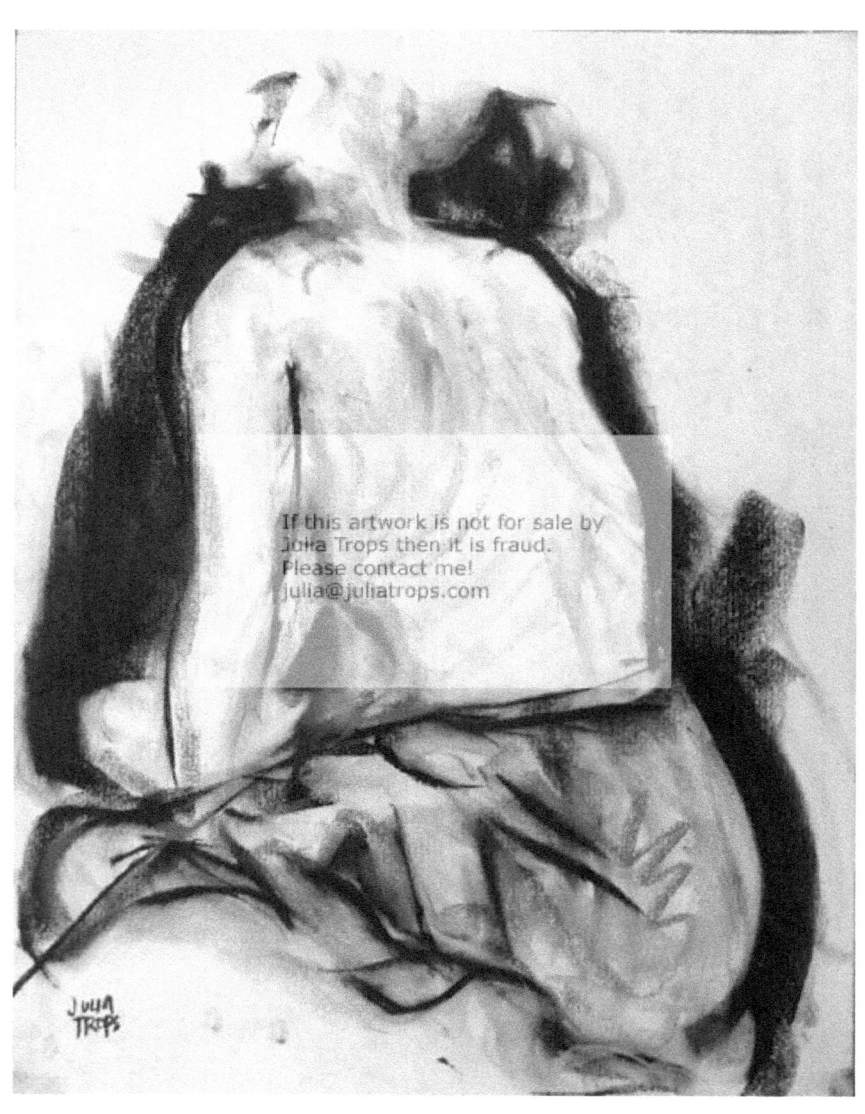

Charcoal and pastels on paper, 24x18

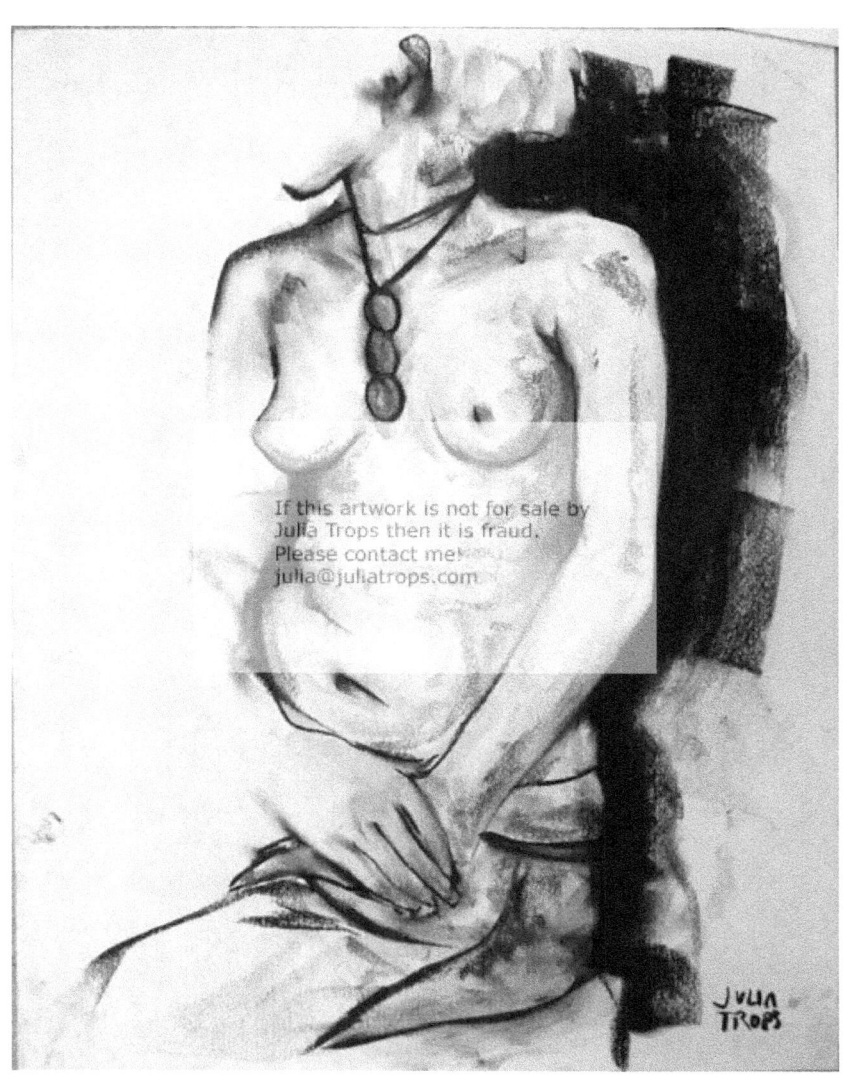

Charcoal and pastels on paper, 24x18

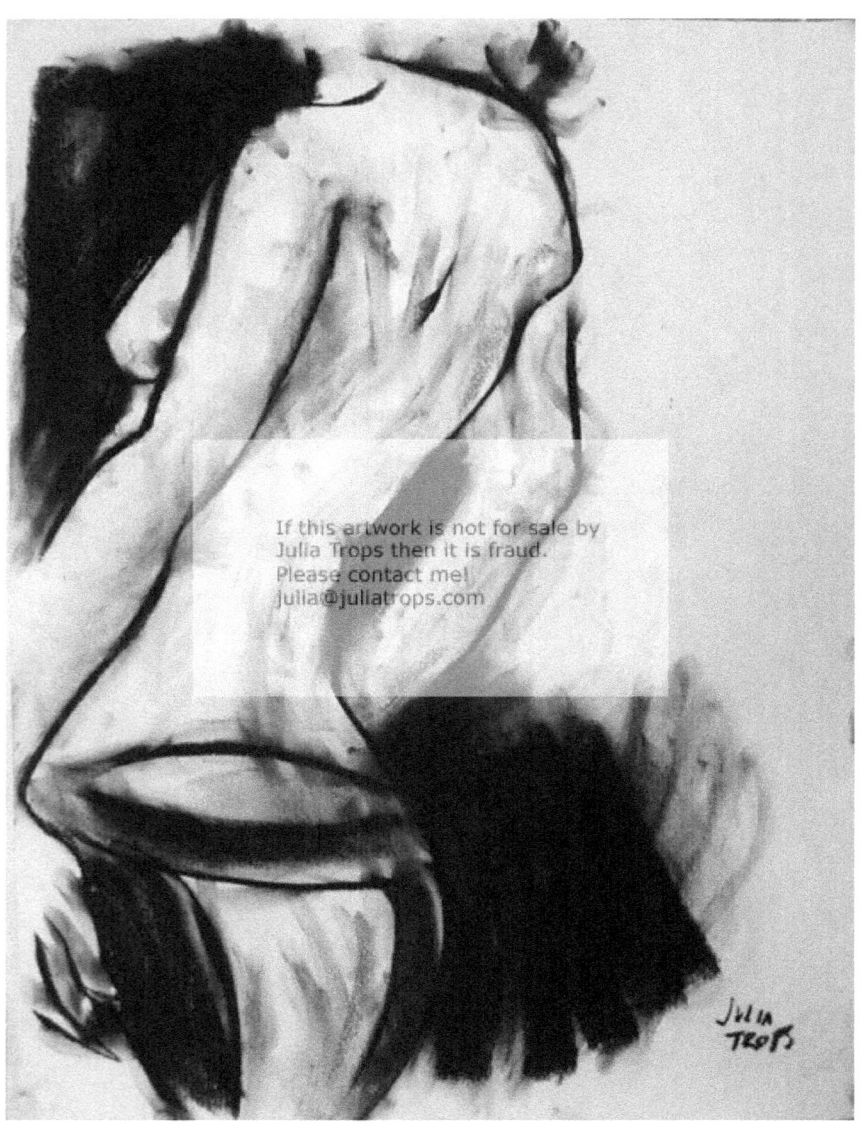

A pose that I enjoy will be repeated as quickly and intensely as possible. If I need to adjust angles of arms or legs, or even their positions, I will do so. I really liked the curve of the

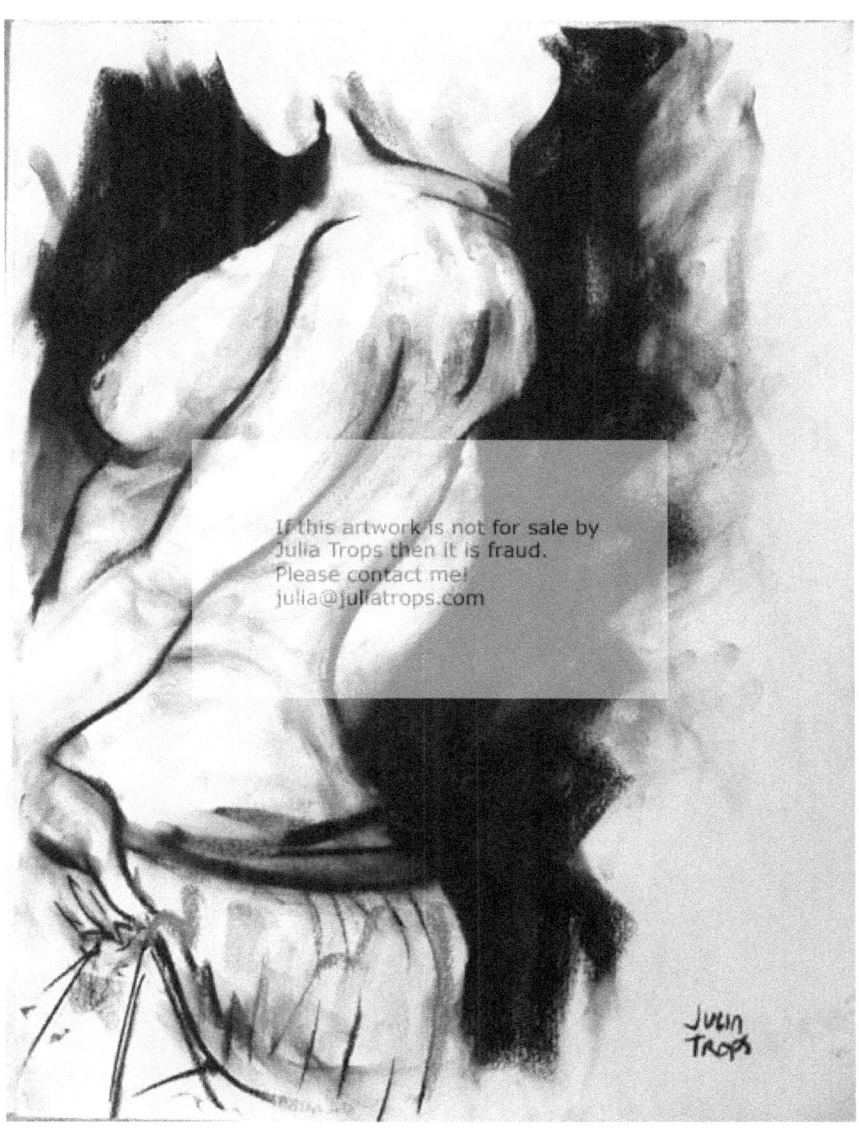

back and the subtle graceful shadows played across the side and hips. Sometimes I will exaggerate form and shape as a sacrifice to expression as you can see in the first drawing.

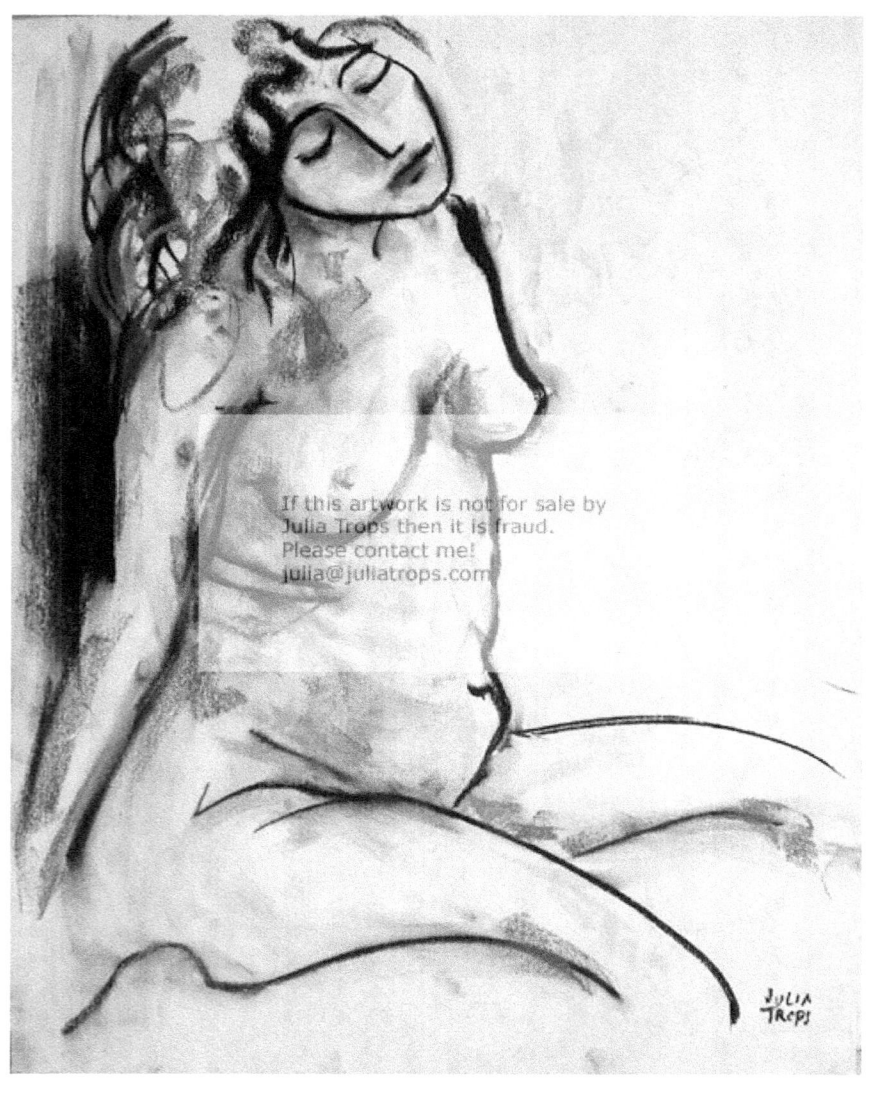

Two drawings of the same pose. The first in a grouping like this can be fairly realistic, the second is a bit more wild and unrestrained, or it works the other way around

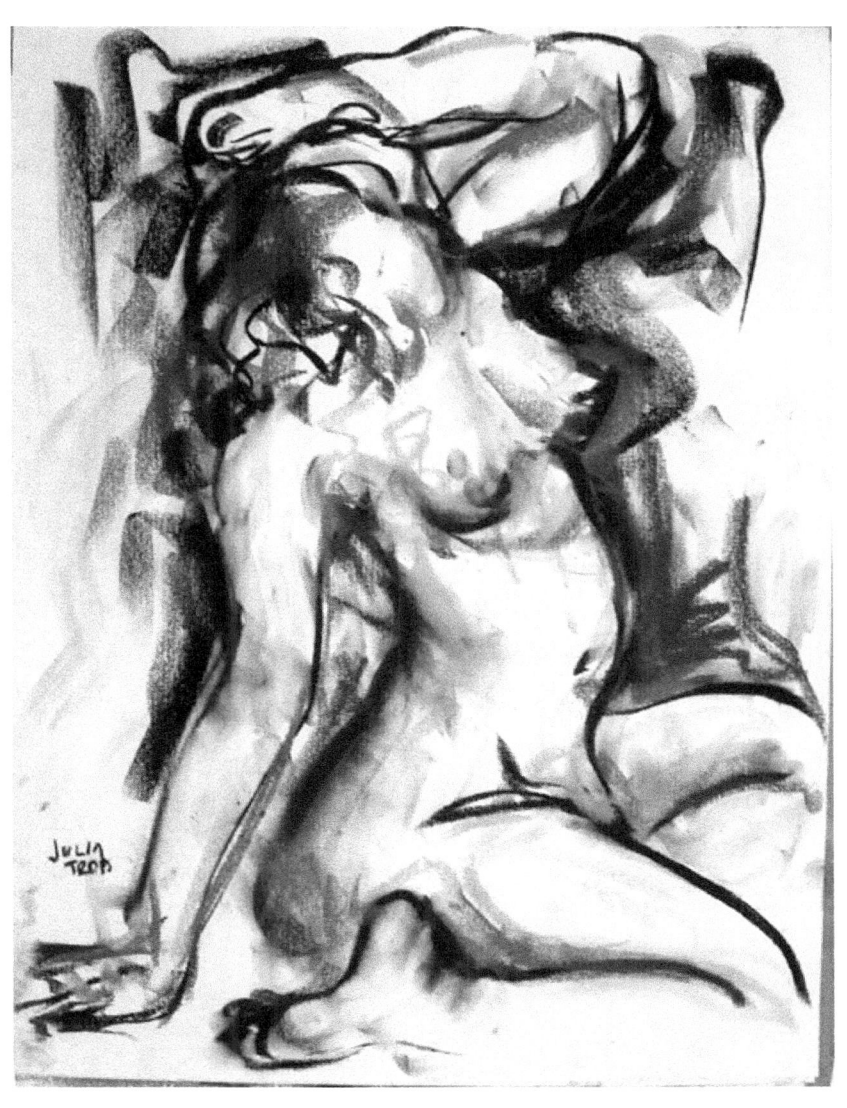

too, depending on how much energy I have at my disposal. It can take a few drawings for it to get calmed down and focussed.

These are examples of a drawing session with Lauren. The goal in these sessions was not to capture realistic form, but to gather the strength and intensity of movement of the medium. Sensuality of strokes, lines, shape and form; an immediate gathering of all senses.

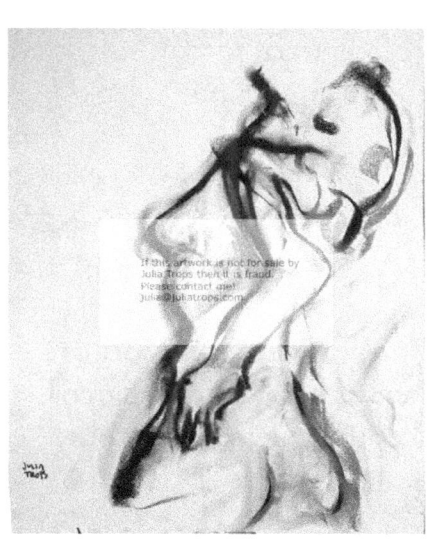
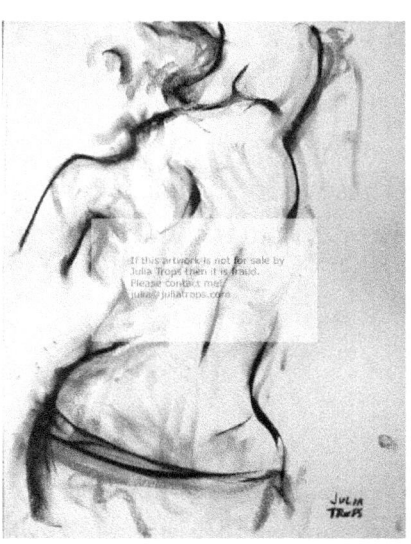
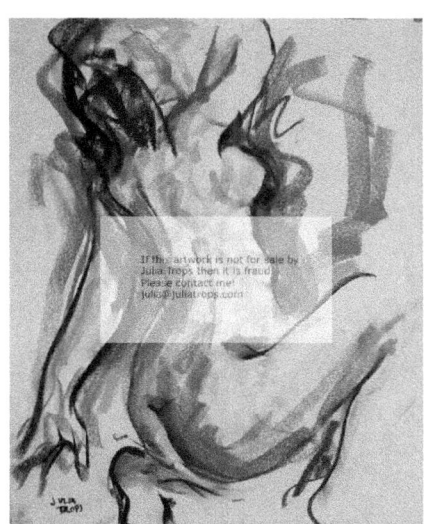
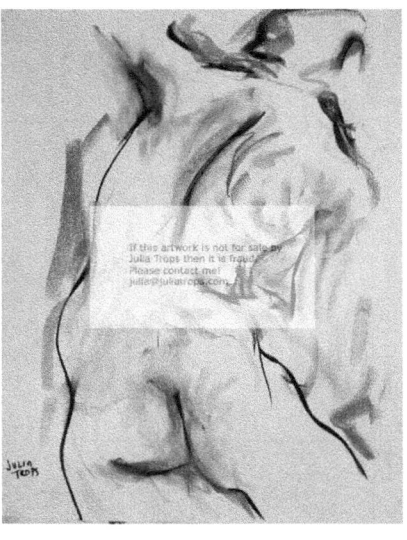

Moving into Paintings

These paintings are translation of charcoal into oils: movement and energy, brushstrokes and colour.

When I do the oils and acrylics, I don't have any sort of preconception of execution. The work is a single charcoal line on a coloured acrylic surface, the palette is laid out, and I paint. Whatever happens, happens.

Much of the time, it is a struggle to name these works, because they are a snapshot of intensity and emotions and time, they are their own beings.

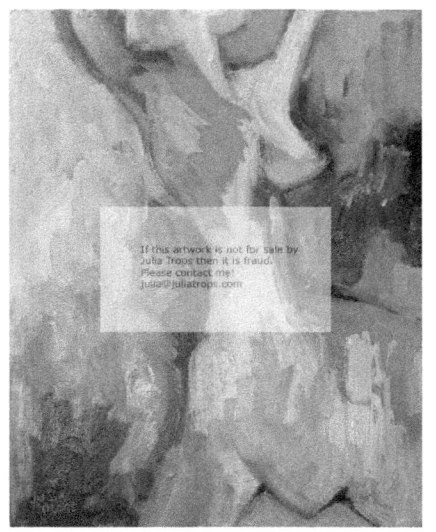
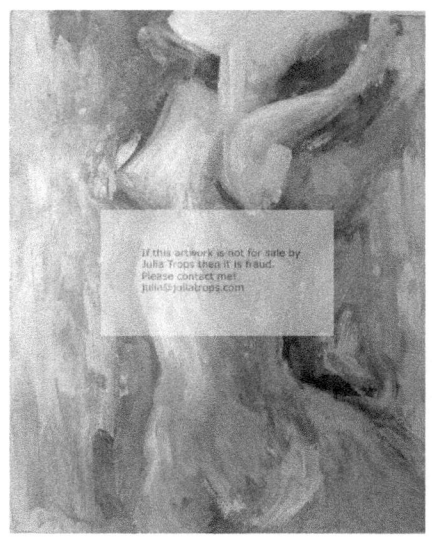
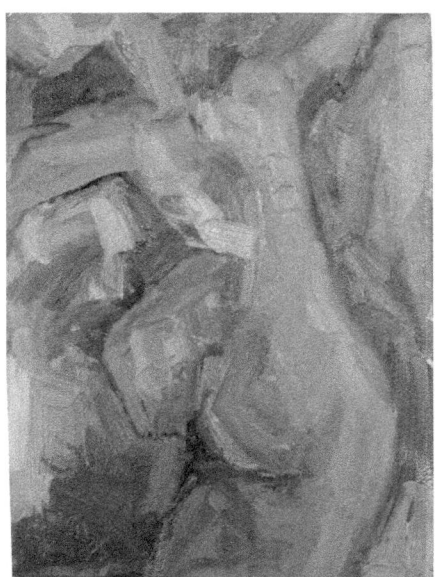
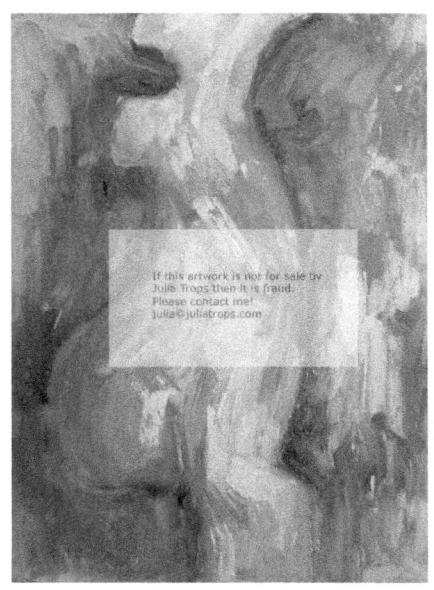

from upper left: Symbolic Speech 14"x11", Adriana's Dance 14"x11", Heloise 8"x6", Way of Noble Love 14"x11"

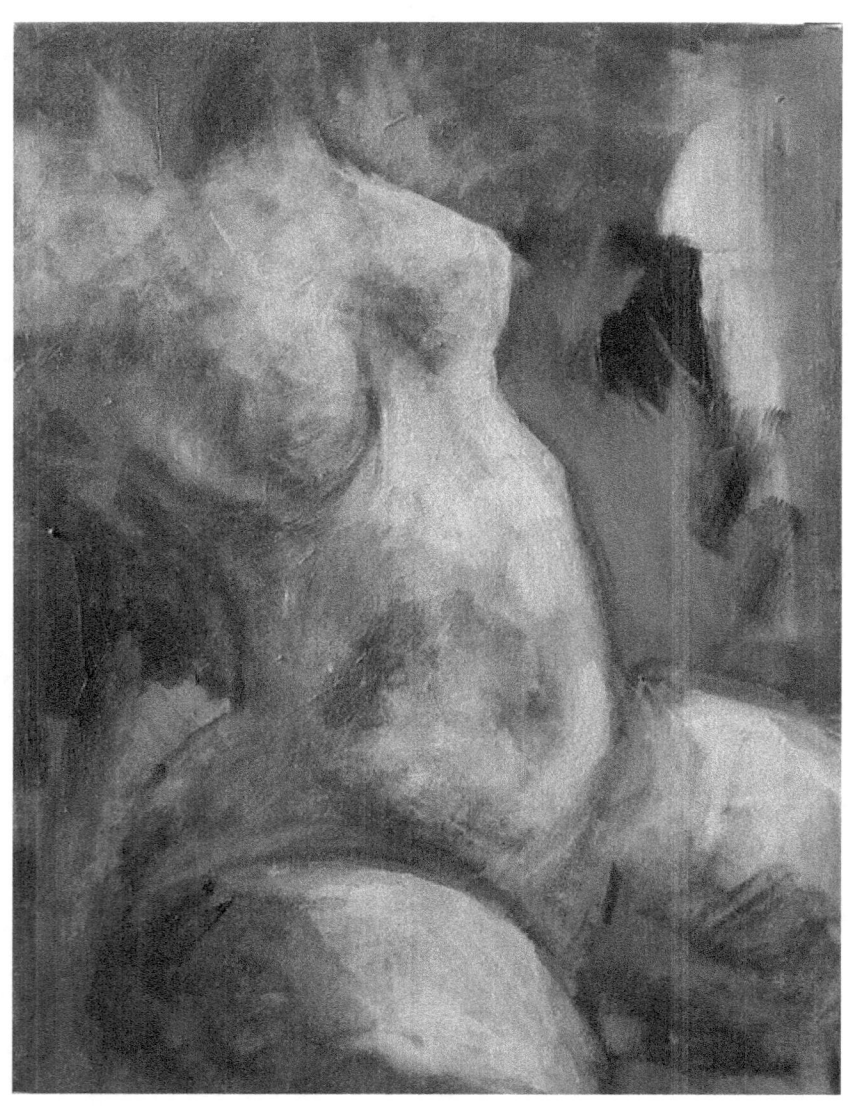

Torso
acrylic on canvas, 14x11

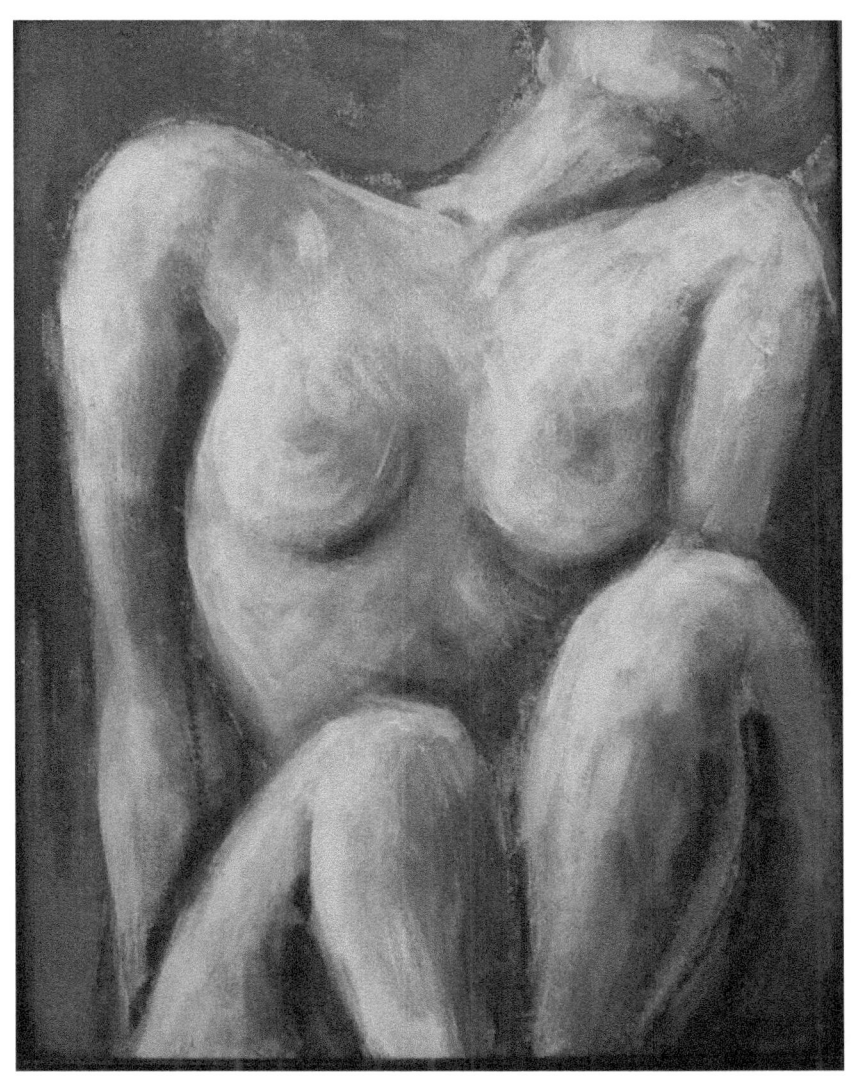

Rapture
acrylic on canvas, 14x11

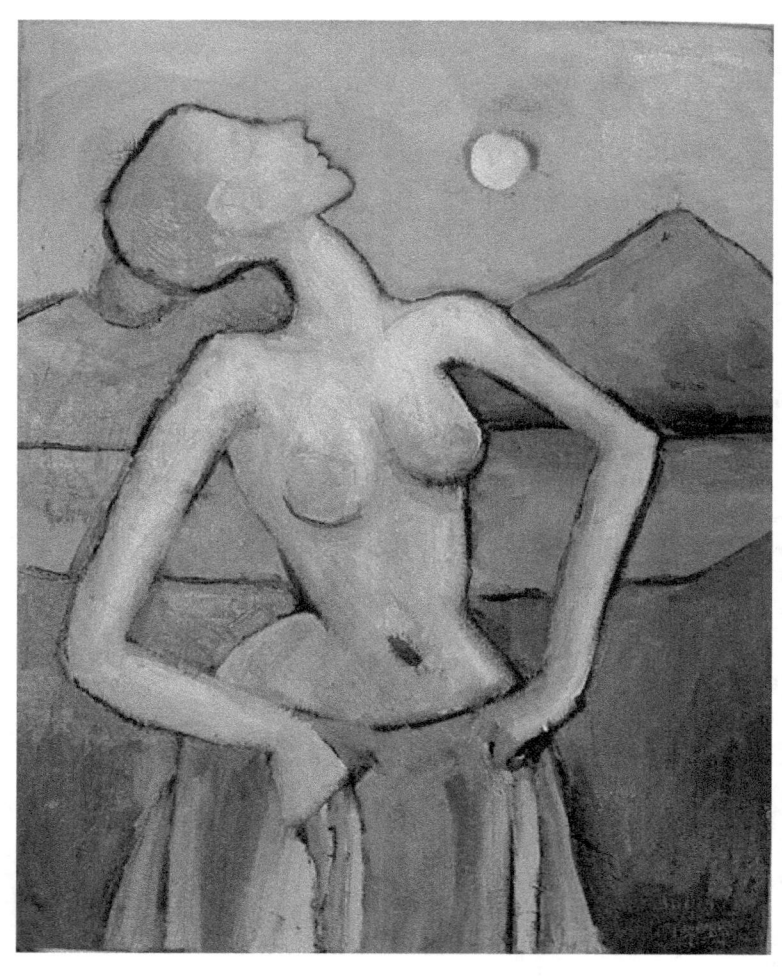

Dancer on the Shore of the Neverending Sun
oil on canvas, 14x11

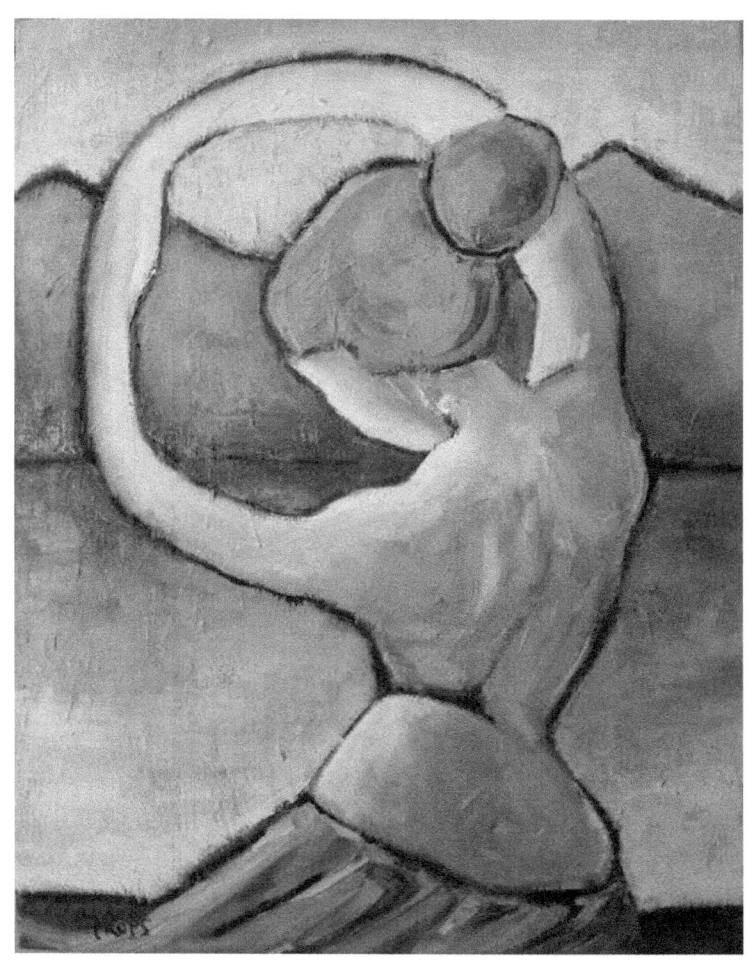

Dancer on the Shore of the Neverending Sun
oil on canvas, 14x11

2009

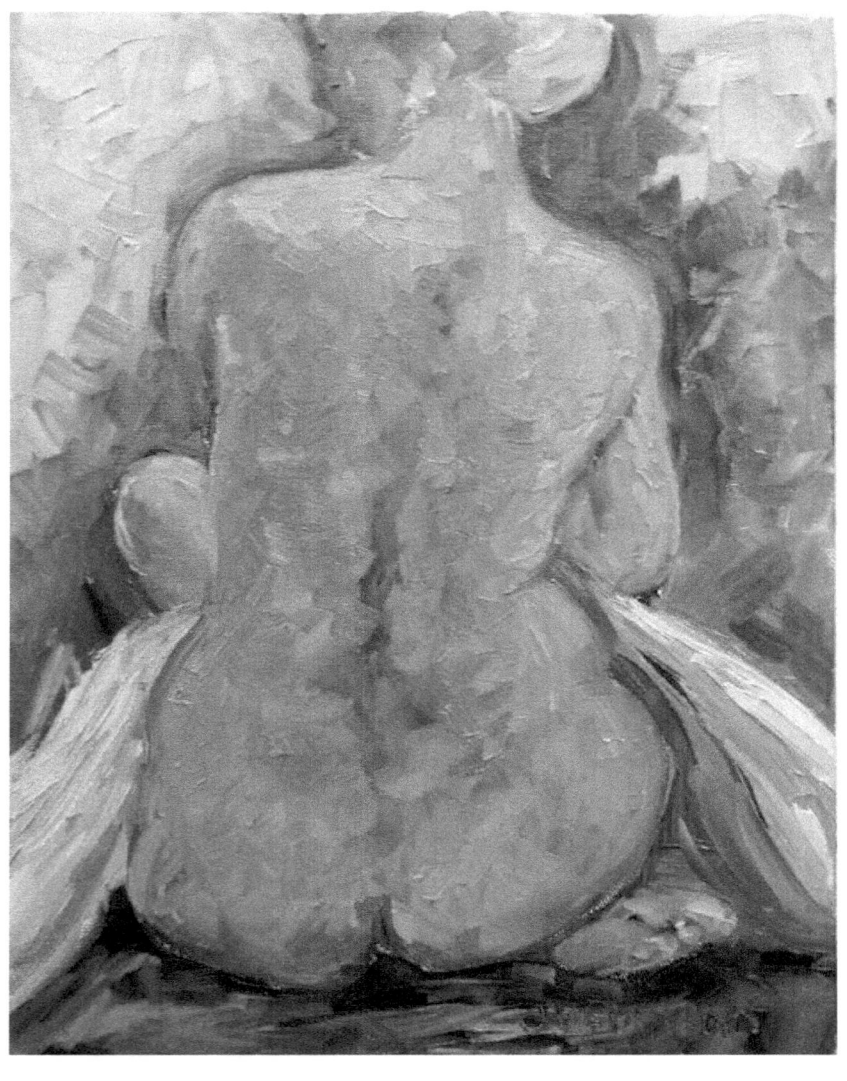

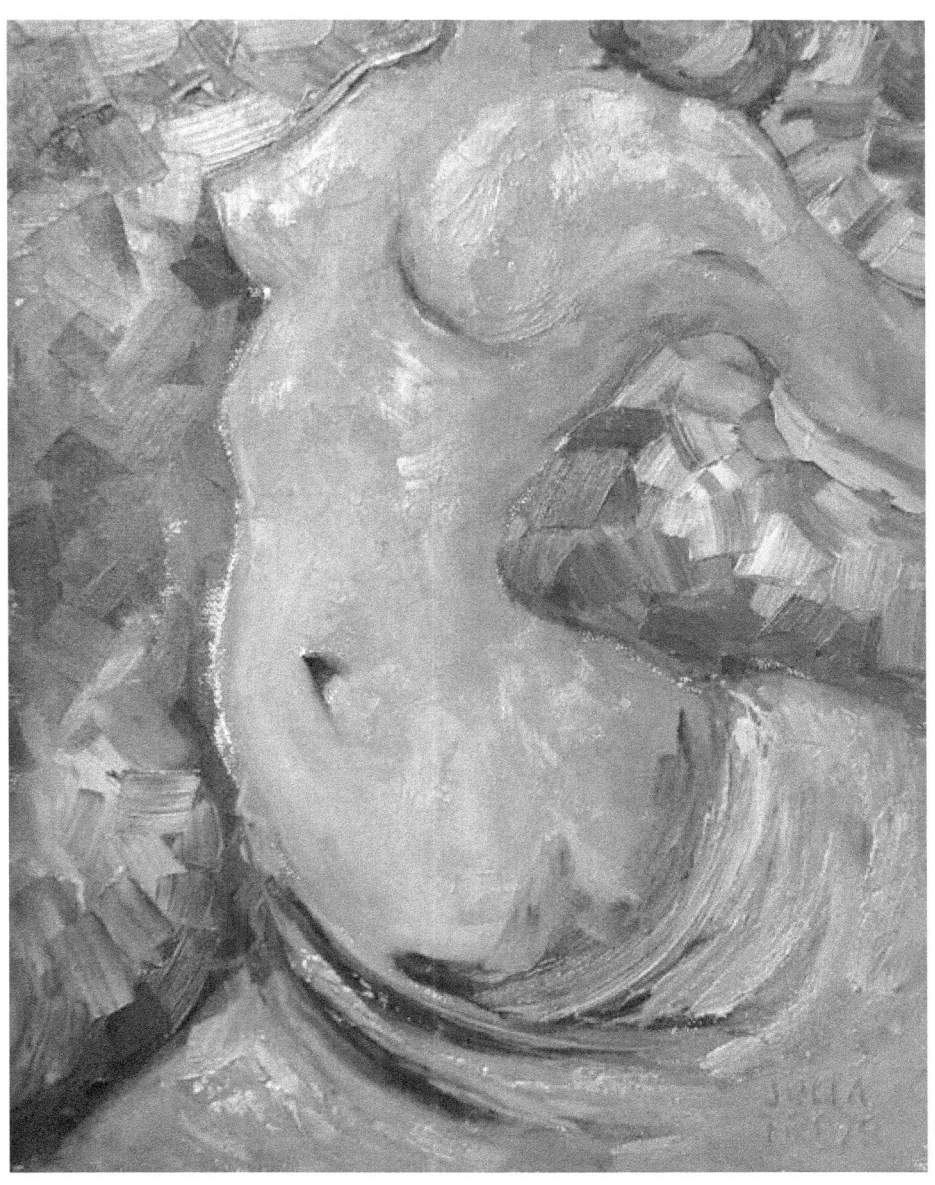

Both of these are cadmium red nudes, oil on canvas, some of the first paintings of the year. The focus was on the emergence of a sensual container of vitality and energy.

To the future...

who knows what the future will bring? My own search for self and identity is enhanced by the knowledge and awareness of others and their experiences. Empathic connections enrich our lives, and I will continue on this road in the execution of my work, whether drawings or paintings or sculpture.

I hope you will follow along with me as I visually explore the vast dual realm of humanness and soulness.

All the best and see you soon!

and lastly....

other scheduled books in the series:

Lauren - Sensuality of Form
Barb - Sophisitication and Grace
Linda - Athletic Femininity
Blake - The Dynamic Essence
Donnalee - The Spiritual Connection
Megan - Goddess of Light
Sandra - Ethereal Dance
Kathryn - Gentle Strength
The Male Collection

and if I can't stop talking, there may be more.

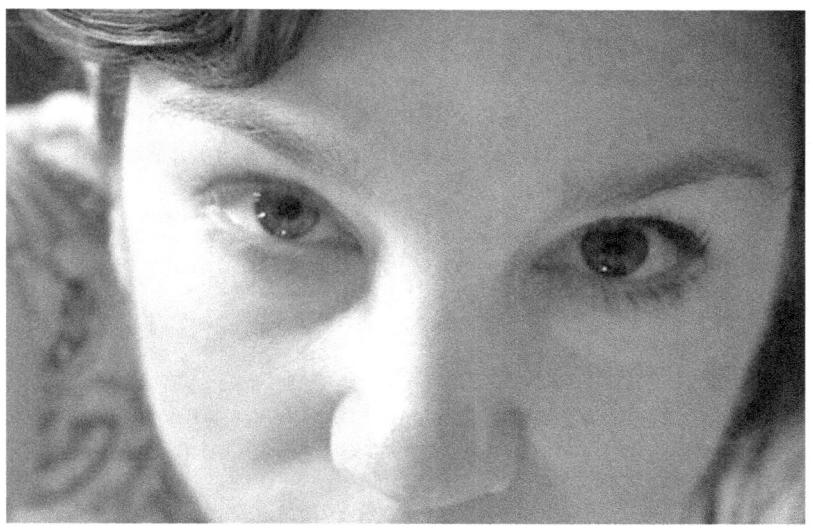

Julia Trops is a Canadian Artist working out of the Rotary
Centre for the Arts in Kelowna BC. Her work focuses on
sensual and sophisticated expressions of the female nude form
in 2D mediums and 3D forms.

You can view her work at her Ruby Lane Shop
http://www.rubylane.com/shops/canadianartist
or email her at juliatrops@gmail.com.

She does accept commissions from time to time. Write her if
you are interested.

Curriculum Vitae

I am a big believer in giving back to the community and I give back in terms of time and passion. The arts community of painters and sculptors, musicians and actors, and their supporters, is very small in Kelowna, and I would dare say, proportionally, a very small group in other centres as well. When we creators pool our resources for the good of the group, we enrich not only our community, but our lives too, which, in turn, enriches our work. It is never a waste of time or love.

Because of this, I have headed up my CV with my community experience rather than my education, and Gallery listings.

Professional & Community Experience
2007 to present- One of three founders for the Okanagan Erotic Art Show
2009 Artist coordinator/curator for Artworks, Evergreen Art Gallery, Rotary Centre for the Arts, Kelowna BC
2008 Artist coordinator/curator for Artworks, Evergreen - Gallerie Diamanté, RCA
2007-9 - Core member establishing the Okanagan Arts Awards
2005 to present - Founding Director for Livessence Society of Figurative Artists and Models, Kelowna, BC
2006 to present - Director Kelowna Museums Society, Kelowna, BC
2005-2007 - Director Arts Council of the Central Okanagan
2002 to present - Resident Artist, Rotary Centre for the Arts, Kelowna BC
2004 Workshops Director and Exhibitions Director, Federation of Canadian Arts - Central Okanagan
2002 to present - Trained life drawing models for instructional and non instructional classes
2001, University of Lethbridge, presented and led topics for discussion in third year "Art Now" classes
2000, Logos and Drawings for Therapist Assistant's Manual for Medicine Hat College, AB
1999, "Assistant" Art Director, CHAT TV, Medicine Hat, AB

Published
2009 - Spirituality of Sex, contributor, coming out October 2009
2009 - Catalog- Okanagan Erotic Art Show, author

Published (continued)
2009 - tba Existence in the Dream
2009 - tba Fluttering of Mozart's Strings
2009 - tba The Model Series (8 or so books, author, artist)
2009 - tba Life Death Becoming
2008 - Spirituality of Music - Mozart painting, page 144
2008 - Spirit of Kelowna Monograph, Introduction
2008 - Wine Labels for The View Winery, Kelowna
2007 - Okanagan Arts Magazine, Article on Donating to Charities (which I turned into a website)
2007 - The Bias Project Catalogue, Edmonton AB
2007 - Exploring Life Drawing by Harold Stone, (isbn 1401896979) contributing artist
and I write my newsletter as well as the one for Livessence.

Galleries
2005 - present Tào Contemporary, Central Hong Kong, Hong Kong
2004 - present Gallery Odin, Silverstar Mountain Resort, BC

Education
2001 - University of Lethbridge Bachelor of Fine Arts - (Art Studio - Painting) Great Distinction
2000 - Medicine Hat College Visual Communications Diploma (Graphic Design) Honours

Listed in
2003 - present National Gallery of Canada's Library and Archives
2004 - present Canada's Cultural Gateway (Government of Canada)
2006- present Saatchi UK Online Gallery

Honours and Awards
2000 - 2001 University of Lethbridge Faculty of Fine Arts Dean's List
2000 Phi Theta Kappa Honour Society Transfer Scholarship & Vice President
1998 - 2000 Medicine Hat College College & President's Honour Roll

Corporate Collections - I am looking to increase my Corporate Collection listings, please contact me! (juliatrops@gmail.com)
2008 - Jigsaw Trading Company, Kelowna, BC
2007 - Bowman Greenhouses, Lake Country, BC

2005 - RBC Dominion Securities, Kelowna, BC
2004 - Cochlear Implant Research Lab, Arizona State University
2004 - Scott-Remlinger, Attorneys-at-law, Atlanta, Georgia, USA

Exhibitions
2009 - Nov-Jun Gallery Odin, Silver Star Resort, BC
2009 - Nov - Evergreen Art Gallery, RCA, Kelowna, BC
2009 - Oct - Kamloops Art Gallery, Kamloops, BC
2009 - Sep - Lake Country Artwalk, Winfield, BC
2009 - Aug - Almost Famous, Gallery Vertigo Vernon, BC
2009 - July - Starry Night, Art Gallery of the South Okanagan, Penticton BC
2009 - Jun-Nov Gallery Odin, Silver Star Resort, BC
2009 - Jun - Okanagan Erotic Art Show, Kelowna, BC
2009 - May - The Bean Scene North, Kelowna, BC
2008 - Dec - The Eclectic Mix, RCA, Kelowna, BC
2008 - Nov-Jun - Gallery Odin Winter Show, Silver Star BC
2008 - Nov - Gallerie Diamanté, Kelowna, BC
2008 - Nov - Livessence Gifts of Colour, Kelowna, BC
2008 - Oct - Gallery Vertigo, Vernon, BC
2008 - Sep to ... Meadowridge Showhomes, Kelowna, BC
2008 - Sep/Oct - The Bean Scene North
2008 - Sep - Lake Country ArtWalk (entered every year fr 2003)
2008 - Aug - Kamloops Art Gallery Fundraiser
2008 - Aug - Gallery Vertigo Almost Famous
2008 - June to Nov - Gallery Odin Summer Show, opening June
2008 - June-Sep - The Best of MASC Geert Maas Sculpture Gardens
2008 - May to Aug - Osoyoos Public Art Gallery
2008 - June - The Works Art and Design Festival - Edmonton
2008 - May to Jul - KCT - People, Places and Things
2008 - May - Rotary Centre for the Arts Atrium
2008 - May - Latitudes - A "Small Art" Show
2008 - April - Okanagan Erotic Art Show
2007 - Kamloops Art Gallery Fundraiser
2007 - Aug - Gallery Vertigo Almost Famous
2007 - The Bias Project The Works Art & Design Festival, Edmonton
2007 - The Works Art and Design Festival Edmonton AB
2007 - Rhythms of Nature, Osoyoos Art Gallery, Osoyoos, BC
2006 - A Year's Work, Galleria, Rotary Centre for the Arts, Kelowna
2005 - Figures! The Old Schoolhouse Gallery, Qualicum Beach, BC
2004 - Alternator Gallery, Kelowna BC

2004 - From Heart to Hearth, Kelowna Art Gallery, BC
2004 - Looking Back, , Kelowna Art Gallery, Kelowna, BC
2003 - Life, Death, Becoming - Galleria, RCA, Kelowna BC
2001 - Graduate Show, University of Lethbridge Art Gallery, Lethbridge
2000 - Chronos/Kronos - Medicine Hat Museum & Art Gallery, Medicine Hat AB

Teaching Experience
2007 - I stopped teaching art with the exception of a few special requests, choosing to focus on my community work, & my artwork
2004-present - Life and Arts Children's Day Instructor
2004-present - Art Instructor for SD23 select teachers
2004 - Beginner Oil Painting - Rotary Centre for the Arts, Kelowna
2003/4 - Beginner and Advanced Instructional Drawing - Rotary Centre for the Arts (Adults and Teens), Kelowna BC
2003/4 - Fundamentals of Art - Rotary Centre for the Arts & selected schools from School District 23 (Child) Kelowna BC
2003/4 - Coordinated Non-instructional Drawing Sessions - Rotary Centre for the Arts
2003 - Drawing Workshop for Mission Painters' Group- 4 weeks

Professional Affiliations
FIDEM - International Medallic Art Society
MASC - Medallic Art Society of Canada
Resident Artist, Rotary Centre for the Arts, Kelowna, BC, 2002-
Director - Kelowna Museums Society, Kelowna, BC 2006-
Director - Arts Council of the Central Okanagan,2006-8
Member - Kelowna Sculptors Network Society - 2008-
Member, Summerland Arts Council - Summerland, BC 2006-
Member - Kelowna Visual Performing Arts Centre Society, 2002-
CARFAC (Canadian Artists' Representation/le Front des artistes canadiens), BC 2003-
Member - Arts Council of the Central Okanagan, 2003-
Vice President, Alpha Tau Delta of Phi Theta Kappa Honour Society Medicine Hat College 1999
Southern Alberta Art Gallery, Lethbridge, AB 2003-
Kelowna Art Gallery, Kelowna, BC 2006-
Alternator Art Gallery, Kelowna, BC 2003-6 2009-

www.ingramcontent.com/pod-product-compliance
Lightning Source LLC
Chambersburg PA
CBHW072251170526
45158CB00003BA/1056